P9-DNF-211

Published by Christian Art Publishers
PO Box 1599, Vereeniging, 1930, RSA

© 2015
First edition 2015

Cover designed by Christian Art Publishers

Images used under license from Shutterstock.com

Scripture quotations are taken from the *Holy Bible,* New International Version® NIV®.
Copyright © 1973, 1978, 1984, 2011 by International Bible Society.
Used by permission of Biblica, Inc.® All rights reserved worldwide.

Scripture quotations are taken from the *Holy Bible,* New Living Translation®.
Copyright © 1996, 2004, 2007, 2013 by Tyndale House Foundation.
Used by permission of Tyndale House Publishers, Inc., Carol Stream, Illinois 60188.
All rights reserved.

Scripture quotations are taken from the New King James Version.
Copyright © 1979, 1980, 1982 by Thomas Nelson, Inc. Used by permission.
All rights reserved.

Printed in China

ISBN 978-1-4321-1488-6

© All rights reserved. No part of this book may be reproduced in any
form without permission in writing from the publisher, except in the case
of brief quotations in critical articles or reviews.

16 17 18 19 20 21 22 23 24 25 – 20 19 18 17 16 15 14 13 12 11

If I settle on the far side of the SEA, even there Your hand will GUIDE me.

Psalm 139:9-10

LET THE SEA & everything in it shout HIS praise!

Psalm 98:7

In high tide or low tide
God will be by your side.

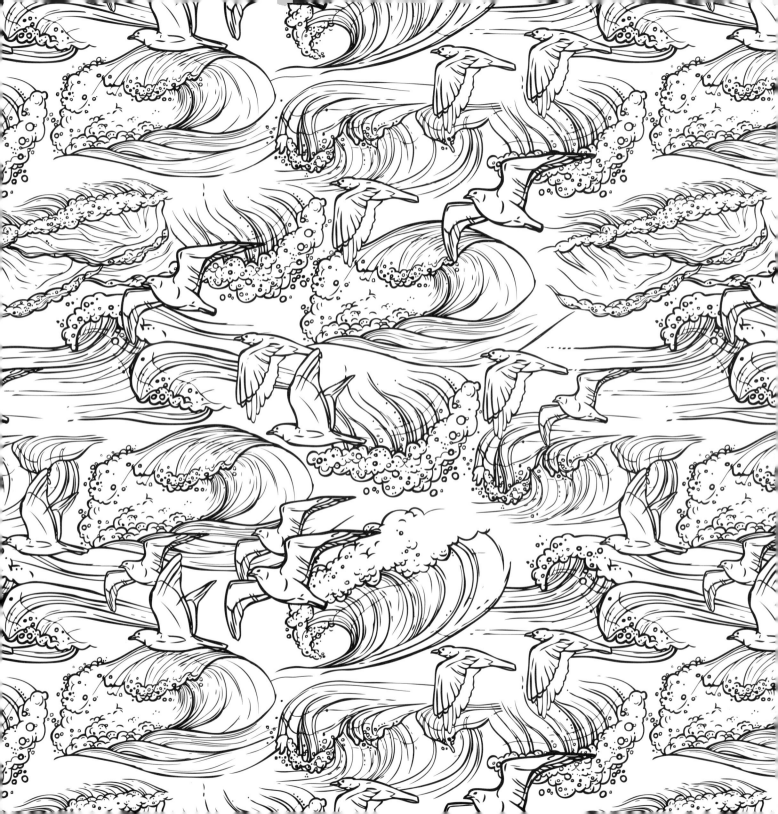

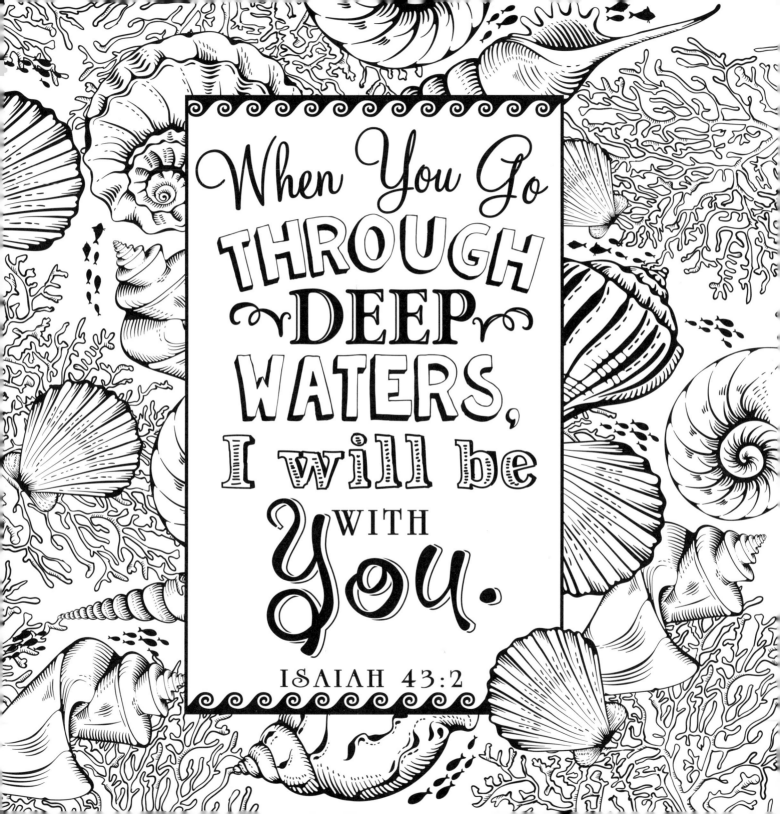

When You Go THROUGH DEEP WATERS, I will be WITH You.

ISAIAH 43:2

FOOTPRINTS

ONE NIGHT I HAD A DREAM.

I WAS WALKING ALONG THE BEACH

WITH THE

LORD

I NOTICED TWO SETS OF

FOOTPRINTS

IN THE SAND.

ONE WAS MINE, AND ONE WAS THE LORD'S

...TO MY SURPRISE

I NOTICED THAT MANY TIMES ALONG THE PATH OF MY LIFE

THERE WAS ONLY ONE SET OF

FOOTPRINTS

THE LORD SAID:

"MY PRECIOUS CHILD

WHERE YOU SEE ONLY ONE SET OF

FOOTPRINTS

IT WAS THEN THAT

I CARRIED YOU."

THE LORD
RESTORES
MY
SOUL.

PSALM 23:3

Hope

IN THE

Lord

Psalm 130:7

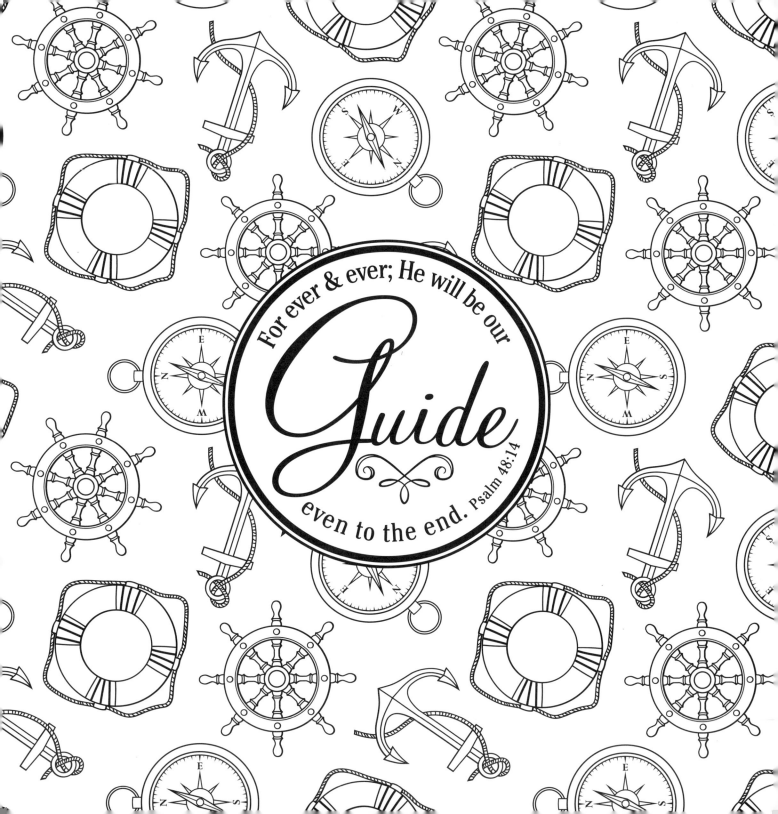

For ever & ever; He will be our *Guide* even to the end. Psalm 48:14

HE WHO DWELLS IN THE SHELTER OF THE MOST High WILL rest IN THE SHADOW OF THE ALMIGHTY

PSALM 91:1

THE LORD KEEPS WATCH OVER YOU

AS YOU COME AND GO,

BOTH NOW AND FOREVER. PSALM 121:8

Cards TO COLOR, CUT & FOLD

Faith. Hope. Love.

Numbers 6:24

May God bless you and keep you.

Blessings!

I Always Thank My God For You.

1 Corinthians 1:4

Thinking of You